GIVING BACK
the
SHAME

Stacey Workman

ISBN 978-1-64515-671-0 (paperback)
ISBN 978-1-64569-647-6 (hardcover)
ISBN 978-1-64515-672-7 (digital)

Christian Faith Publishing, Inc.
832 Park Avenue
Meadville, PA 16335
www.christianfaithpublishing.com

Printed in the United States of America

I will repay you for the years
the locusts have eaten—

Joel 2:25 (NIV)

Chapter 1

Dad

It was all so fascinating! Here I was on what I thought of as my first big outing into the world! Downtown at the Ice Capades! The ice-skating, the music, all the people—I was so enthralled. When it was over, we were walking out through the lobby, and Mom told me to hang on to her purse strap as we headed toward the door. Then I saw them—a whole big bunch of shiny balloons shaped like airplanes, so yellow and sparkly. They were so beautiful and mesmerizing I wanted a better look, so I stopped walking and just stared at them. After what seemed like only a minute, I realized I was no longer holding on to Mom's purse, so I turned to grab it but Mom wasn't there...

A small ball of panic began to form in the pit of my stomach. I didn't know what to do at first. Then I thought that I would just meet them out at the car... Then I remembered that you had dropped us off at the front of the arena and then parked, so I didn't know where the car was.

There was another couple with us, so I stood and turned in a circle hoping to find at least one of four familiar faces. As I slowly spun, seeing no one I knew, a feeling of dread crept in and joined the increasing panic. And it wasn't because I thought I was lost. It was because I knew I was going to pay for letting go of Mom's purse. There was going to be pain. And the longer it took for me to be found, the worse the punishment would be. There were still a lot of people around me, so I thought I would go stand outside on the sidewalk. Maybe I could see and be seen better out there.

So I slowly started walking toward the doors. With every step, that ball of panic grew bigger and up into my throat. When I reached the sidewalk, I stood and waited, trying not to cry. A moment later, a woman came up to me and asked me if I was lost. It was taking every fiber of my small body to fight back the fear and the tears, and all I could do was give a small nod. I don't know why I nodded because I knew wasn't lost, not really. What I was, was doomed.

If I could have spoken, I would have begged you to take me with you. You had such a nice face, and the tone of your voice said you were really concerned about me. I could tell that you wouldn't blame me or hit me and that I would be safe with you. I imagined you taking me to your house and sitting me down in your warm pale-yellow kitchen and making me some hot chocolate while you told me that you were glad I wasn't hurt and that it wasn't my fault. That I was too young to be responsible for my safety and that you would never be careless with me. But, with great sadness, I put the brakes on that wishful thinking. Why continue dreaming of a happy outcome knowing that it was absolutely pointless? No amount of wishing or hoping was going to save me from the monster in my father's clothing.

That nice lady put her hand on my shoulder and looked out toward the parking lot, and I followed her gaze. Almost immediately, I saw you stomping toward me with your vise-grip hands balled into fists and a murderous look on your face. As you got closer and closer, my insides solidified with fear, and I'm pretty sure I stopped breathing. When you reached me, you didn't even glance at the woman who was trying to help me—trying to keep me safe. You were boiling over with rage that was completely focused on me. Immediately, you got right in my face and started yelling. Hot waves of anger washed over me, and with every word, spit flew from your lips and landed on my face, but I was too paralyzed with fear to wipe it away, swallowed by your enormous wild eyes and the death grip you had on my arm. Then you turned, jerking me along with you, and headed toward the car. I had to run or else be dragged behind you.

The next thing I remember is the five of us sitting in some restaurant. I didn't want any food. Just the thought of eating made me want to throw up. I was afraid you were going to force me to eat. But fortunately, you didn't.

So, I sat there while everyone else was eating, thinking, Why in the world are we even here at this restaurant?

I could tell that no one wanted to be there. They all just looked down at their plates as they ate and didn't say a word. Except you, Dad. In between bites, you'd glare at me with those terrifying angry eyes and say, not quietly, "You're lucky you're sitting here right now!"

Another bite, then...

"You've had it when we get home!"

Another bite...

"Be glad you're sitting here and not at home!"

A bite...

"You are gonna get it!"

You kept going on and on the whole time we were in the restaurant. And I was pretty sure that most, if not all of the other people there, could hear you as well. That didn't seem to bother you at all. And none of the other adults at our table said a word about how loud you were. It was as if they were afraid you would punish them like you were going to punish me. And with every bellowed comment, I felt my face grow hotter and hotter with embarrassment and shame.

My brain raced…
There are three other grown-ups here. Why won't anyone help me? You know what's going to happen to me. I know you all know! Why aren't you doing anything? Why won't anyone do something? Why won't anyone save me?

My silent pleas went unanswered as I sat there, immobile, bound by his fury and my humiliation.

I don't understand… Am I really so bad? I'm only five and already such a terrible person that my own father wants to hurt me. Am I really too much of a burden that my own mother won't do or say anything to help me? Why is this happening to me? What's wrong with me?

I sat there silently, looking down at my hands on my lap while the grown-ups ate, trying to make myself as small as possible.

Wishing with all my heart and soul that I could just melt into the chair and just disappear. The whole time hoping that you wouldn't suddenly decide to start punishing me right there in the restaurant in front of all those people. That was the longest and shortest dinner of my life.

Then we were in the car heading home. I was sitting in the back pinned to the seat by the weight of your anger that permeated the entire car. I couldn't hear, I couldn't think, and I couldn't breathe. All I could do was stare at the back of the driver's seat as I rode toward my doom.

In the blink of an eye, the car was pulling into our driveway. The last thing I wanted to do was get out of the car, but I knew I had no choice. And I knew that if I tried to delay, it would just make you angrier. So, fearfully, I followed you and Mom into the house through the breezeway. Once inside the house, I stood for a moment, staring at the basement door, unsure if I should enter the living room on the left or the kitchen on the right. Either way led to the front end of the hallway where the attic door was. And in front of the attic door was where you stood and yelled for me to get over there.

As I walked through the kitchen toward you, I could hear the slide of your belt as you yanked it through the loops of your jeans. You grabbed me roughly, jerked down my pants and underwear, and began to thrash me with your belt as hard as you could. The first blow felt like a thousand wasps all stinging me at the same time. The second blow felt like a million. After that, my entire body was racked with a burning, gut-wrenching pain from the surface of my skin to the pit of my stomach as your vicious strikes landed not only on my bottom but on my back and legs. I didn't think it was ever going to end. I could sense your rage and resentment with every swing of your arm that was punctuated by booming, high-pitched comments.

"How do you like that?"

WHACK!

"Are you going to do that again?"

WHACK!

"How does that feel?"

WHACK!

"Huh?"

WHACK! WHACK! WHACK! WHACK! WHACK!

Then suddenly, there was nothing—no light, no sound, and no air. I slowly opened my eyes and discovered it was morning, and I was in my bed in my pajamas. I couldn't remember how I got there. Was I alive? Then I sat up and knew that I was still alive because the entire backside of my body was aching—like it was covered with one enormous bruise that reached down to my bones.

You had whipped me so brutally that I blacked out. The pain had become so agonizing that my brain had had no other choice but to shut down in order to survive.

How could you treat your own child that way? After you found me, not once did you ask if I was hurt or if I was scared. All you cared about was how *you* felt. Were you ever even afraid for me? Was there just one second of fear that your daughter could be gone forever? And instead of being grateful and happy that I was unharmed, you became furious. Why? I was only five! And instead of being concerned about my safety, you punished me for pissing you off!

Something inside me broke after that. I felt it. Like a huge chunk of my soul had been chiseled off.

It was summertime, and I was playing down the street with a couple neighborhood kids at their house. Usually when we were there, we played outside, and I could hear you yell my name at dinnertime. This particular day we were playing inside, and I didn't hear you calling me. I happened to glance at the clock and saw it was about fifteen minutes past dinnertime. I was late.

Oh no! I gotta go home now!

I jumped up, ran out of the house, grabbed my bike that was lying in the driveway, and headed out to the street. My heart was beating so hard and fast I was sure that at any moment, it was going to burst right out of my chest. When I got to the street, there you were—standing at the end of the driveway huffing and puffing with that wild wide-eyed look on your face. Biting your tongue like you always do when you get mad. I looked down, and in your right hand was the paddle.

That hateful paddle you made just for your children. You had carved it out of a one-by-three—about three feet long with a nice sturdy handle. You even cared enough to sand it, stain it, and clear coat it. You were so proud of it.

Instantly I was in a five-alarm panic! I jumped on my bike and began to peddle toward the house. But in that direction the street was uphill, and I had trouble gaining momentum. I had to stand and pedal to get going. The moment I stood you started hitting me with that paddle.

I thought if I could get up enough speed, I could get away from you. But the harder I pedaled, the slower I seemed to go. With every smack of that paddle, my legs grew heavier and heavier. I even looked down at my feet to make sure they hadn't turned into concrete blocks. You kept up with me the whole way.

"Get your ass moving!"

WHACK!

"You know when to be home!"

WHACK!

WHACK!

"This is what you get for not listening to me!"

WHACK!

WHACK!

You hit me so hard that a few times I almost fell of my bike.

If that had happened, I'd have really been in for it. I had every reason to believe that if I had fallen, you would've just started beating me with that board as I lay in a heap in the middle of the street.

I didn't see any neighbors out, but there were cars in the driveways, so I knew they were home. At least a few of them had to have been alerted to what was happening—you kept screaming while you were hitting me.

So now, along with the pain and fear, there was humiliation. And that humiliation was a hundred times worse than your hardest hit. Because now everyone we knew could see how horrible I was and how much you hated me. I could feel my face turning as red as my bike.

The road we were on was a main thoroughfare through that part of town, and cars always flew at least forty-five miles an hour or more in both directions. Oh, how I passionately wished that one of those cars would hit me and kill me. But of course, not one single car came by.

It was around an eighth of a mile back to our house, but it may as well have been ten. I didn't think I was going to survive. But then I saw it. The two-story brick house next door to our house. It had a row of hedges about five feet high separating the front yard from the road. Our driveway was just after those hedges... I was almost home.

Not that I would necessarily be safe there, but at least the neighbors wouldn't be able to see...

Once we reached the hedges, you stopped hitting me. So I jumped off my bike and ran with it. I knew you could start swinging that board again at any moment, so I ran as fast as I possibly could past the farmhouse and up our driveway. When I reached the house, I quickly parked my bike in the driveway and raced through the door into the kitchen. I immediately sat in my chair at the dark brown wooden oval table.

Dinner was a very quiet affair that evening. The tension was so thick that even my little brother, who was normally rather chatty, stayed quiet. I kept my head bent down over my plate for most of it. On the occasions when I did dare to glance up you were glaring at me. Reminding me of the terrible thing I just did and to never stop being afraid of you.

••◆►——————◆——————◄◆••

That's how I lived my life—in fear. Terror, actually. Because I knew that at any given moment, all hell could break loose. At first, I wasn't sure what could potentially send you into a rage. Quickly, I learned that anything and everything could be a trigger—big or small—like those crappy drinking glasses that one of the fast food restaurants used to give away. Those things were as thin as a sheet of paper.

One night, as I was washing the dinner dishes, one of those glasses bumped against the side of the sink and cracked. Your eyes went wide, your face turned red, and you flew into a rage. You acted like I had just shattered an entire collection of irreplaceable china. You were yelling and swearing about how I couldn't do anything right and that I ruined everything. I didn't say a word—to do so would risk getting the paddle. All I wanted was to finish those dishes as fast as possible and get out of the kitchen. But I couldn't risk another broken glass, so I was forced to move slowly. Time seemed to stop as I stood at the sink fighting back the tears. Tears, of course, would make things even worse.

Finally, I finished and took off running to my room. I curled up on my bed and let out the tears that I had been fighting to hold back.

Why did I break that glass? How could I be so stupid? So worthless? Why was a cheap drinking glass with a silly clown on it more valuable than me?

It was the most innocuous things that pissed you off the most. A noise, spilt milk, a question, or a misplaced TV Guide—that only you used—was enough to make me fear for my life. Whenever something enraged you,

there always had to be someone to blame—
someone to punish. And that person was
almost always me. Even if I was nowhere near
the house, the moment I walked through the
door you'd start.

"This is your fault!"

"How can it be my fault? I wasn't even
here."

"Because you're the oldest! And you
should have been here! If you were here, this
wouldn't have happened!"

I had no choice but to stand there and
take it every time as piece after piece of my
soul flew away.

And nothing was ever an accident as
far as you were concerned. I had to have
an answer for everything. And it didn't matter what the actual truth was. What mattered
was that you heard the words you *wanted* to
hear—what you considered to be the "right"
answer. And you had better hear the words
you wanted to hear or else! So I had to antic-
ipate any and all questions that could come
out of your mouth—which could be absolutely
anything—and come up with the hopefully
acceptable answers. I never knew when or
where you would snap, but I did know I had to
be constantly ready with answers. In order to
do that, my brain had no choice but to function

in a perpetual state of hypervigilance—on high alert 24/7—to try to protect myself.

•••••━━━━━━•━━━━━━•••••

You and I were sitting at the kitchen table in the late afternoon. I was eight years old. You were to my left and an open window behind you filled the kitchen with soft sunlight as a tepid breeze flowed around us. While you were leafing through a car magazine, and I had my sixty-four-pack of crayons and a coloring book. We sat there for a while, calmly and silently, absorbed in our activities. Then you made a casual comment like you were thinking out loud, "Liver sounds good for dinner."

With my head still down over my coloring book, I casually commented back, "Yuck, I don't want liver."

A split second later, the sunlight and the breeze were gone, and I looked up to see why. Less than inch from my face was your wild-eyed face, and I remember thinking how surprised I was that we didn't smack heads when I looked up. I felt little drops of spittle hit my face as you said, in the lowest but fiercest voice I'd ever heard,

"I don't care what you want."

And just as quickly as your face had appeared, it disappeared—back to your magazine.

Wordlessly, I turned my head back down to my coloring book but did not pick up a crayon. I sat, staring unseeingly at the half-colored page, completely baffled, trying to figure out your unprovoked and cruel declaration.

My little-kid brain came to the conclusion that "I don't care what you want" really meant that my feelings didn't matter—they meant nothing. And if my feelings meant nothing, then my existence as a human being meant nothing.

••●■————————●————————■●••

One evening, when I was in junior high, you left the house by yourself after dinner. When I finished helping Mom clean up, I sat down on the living floor to watch some TV. A while later, you came home. The first thing you did was walk up to me and hand me a small white rectangular box. I looked at the box, looked up at you, then looked back down at the box in my hand.

I sat there holding the box—stunned.

You're giving me a gift? For no reason? What the hell is going on? You can't stand me. All I've done is ruin your life, and you've bought me something?

I wasn't sure what to do at first, and then I realized you were waiting for me to open the box. So I slowly lifted the lid. Inside was a watch. It had a white face and a white silicone band. On the right side of the face was a pink flamingo. Behind the flamingo were water and two green palm trees. Now I was even more confused. Not only had you bought me something out of the blue—but why this particular watch? It's tropical and girlie, and that's not my style.

As I sat there, staring at the watch, trying to figure it out, you said, "It was the only one that had green in it, and green is your favorite color."

Good thing I was already sitting because those words would have knocked me right over.

You know my favorite color? And you took the time to find something for me with that color in it? Are you feeling all right?

Thank you. Say thank you, my brain told me. But I couldn't. It was as if my jaw had been wired shut, and my voice had dried up. All I could do was look back and forth from the watch to you with my brow slightly furrowed as

I tried to process what was happening. Then you walked out of the living room while I sat there stunned.

Oh, how I absolutely loved that watch! And I loved you for buying it for me. It was evidence that you didn't altogether hate me. And maybe you had just a little love for me.

And oh, how I absolutely hated that watch! And I hated you for buying it for me. I hated it for the exact same reason I loved it. I was taking great pains to forget about the love I had for you. So far, I had managed to bury it pretty far down. It brought me only heartache. And it was much easier to endure your abuse as long as I thought you didn't love me. Because if you did love me, I'd be unable to take it.

That act of kindness allowed a portion of my love for you to bubble up and break through the surface. Then my survival instincts set in, and I was able to stomp that love back down where it belonged.

⸻

Growing up, I lived in unremitting fear and stress. The fear became so intense that if you were in the living room, I had to lie flat on the floor and crawl on my stomach down the hallway from my bedroom to go to the bathroom. From any seat in the living room, you could see the bathroom door, and I was deathly afraid of crossing your line of sight. To do so could unleash on me any malevolence that was roiling around in your head. Then, after using the bathroom and hoping the flush of the toilet wouldn't betray me, I would get back down on my stomach and slowly and fearfully crawl back down the hallway to my bedroom, heart pounding, grateful that I had made it back unscathed.

The stress became so bad that, for a period of time, I heard voices. More specifically, your voice when you weren't anywhere near the house. I'd be alone in my room sitting on my bed, reading, or listening to my boom box when suddenly I'd hear you bellow my name,

"STACEY!"

in that staccato tone that meant I was in big, big trouble. And it was so loud I'd have sworn you were standing right next to me. And in a flash, I would spring off the bed onto the floor. And I'd stand there gasping and shaking. My hypervigilance kicking into overdrive, trying to brace myself for whatever hell was about to rain down, while staring at my bedroom door expecting to hear your footsteps pounding down the hall. But there were no footsteps. The only thing I could hear was my heart pounding frantically. On one hand, I was thankful because I wasn't in danger. On the other, I wasn't very happy because hearing your voice, clear as a bell, when you weren't there, was not good.

I stood there for a moment or two longer just to make sure I was still alone. Then I picked my book up off the floor, climbed back onto the bed, and continued reading. I kept one ear cocked for more voices, but I heard nothing else...that day.

Every time I found myself alone and immersed in something—usually a book—your voice would return. Always, it was the same as the first time—your loud staccato voice screaming my name, sounding like you were right next to me. And every time I'd jump a mile into the air, heart racing, scared to death. It was always so real.

I know, because you told me numerous times, that you blamed me for almost everything because I was the oldest child. But I always felt that there was more to it than that. I believed that you also blamed me for almost everything because I was an accident. Born approximately ten months after you and Mom were married, and you resented me for it.

Decades later, my suspicions were confirmed. You looked me right in the eyes and said, "Yes, you were an accident. We wanted more time together alone as a married couple before we had kids. But I still love you."

Really? You "still love" me? What a crock.

•••••━━━━━━━━━•━━━━━━━━━••••

I have no idea where your rage came from. I do know that you had more than one choice in dealing with that rage. For whatever reason. you chose violence. And your brand of violence, more than all the others combined, chipped at my soul until my humanness was all but annihilated.

Chapter 2

The Price of
Friendship

We met on the bus to school toward the end of my first grade year. You were in one of the last seats in the back, and I sat in the seat in front of you. We talked a bit and found that we got along and started hanging out sometimes—mostly on the weekends. We didn't catch the bus at the same stop, but you lived close enough that I could ride my bike or walk to your house—a split level with light blue siding. Behind the house was a small yard that led to some woods that stretched back behind and out on both sides of the house. In the middle of the woods was a creek where we hung out a lot unless the weather was bad. On those days, we would hang out in your basement.

The basement had a full-sized bed in the left back corner. Along the back wall were shelves containing quite a few books, games, and toys. In the middle of the room was an old round wooden kitchen table painted brown with a couple of matching square spindle chairs. In front of that was a long faded green

Berber couch that faced the front wall. I had matching couch pillows on both ends and a couple worn blankets thrown over the back. In front of the couch was a light brown coffee table with nicks all over the top. Just beyond that, against the front wall, a large console television that no longer worked.

One afternoon, it was too humid and buggy to be outside, so we were hanging out in the basement where it was much cooler. You said you didn't feel like playing a board game. You wanted to do something different. You told me to climb on the bed. So I got on the bed and knelt in the middle.

I thought were we gonna jump? Maybe play trampoline or something?

Then you climbed onto the bed and got on your knees in front of me. You pulled your shorts down to just below your hips and said, "Touch it." I looked at you, my brow furrowed in confusion, and said, "I don't want to."

"Come on, touch it."

"No."

You kept asking and asking…cajoling, pleading. And still I said no.

Then you threatened me. Threatened to not talk to me anymore…to not be my friend anymore.

Please, not that! You are the only friend I have! The only escape I have from my house. So, okay, I'll touch you…just please don't stop being my friend!

I wasn't sure why you wanted me to touch you there. All I knew was that that was where the pee came out. Yuck. But one friend was better than no friend. So, I looked at you, gave a small sigh, reached out, and took you in my hand. Your hips began to move slowly back and forward. And your eyes closed as your head tilted back. I began to see that there was more to that part of the body than I thought. You were enjoying what was happening. When you told me to take off my shorts, I hesitated for a moment but then obeyed. I wondered if I would feel good down there, too. But when you touched me, I felt nothing. So I moved my hips like you did—still nothing. I was puzzled. Why did it feel good for you and not for me? Was it because you were older than me? But I didn't say anything because I didn't want you to get mad at me.

When you were done, we put our shorts back on, and I left. Slowly, I walked up the narrow side street lined on both sides by tall maple trees with the occasional house tucked in. As I made my way home, I thought about what had happened.

Was what we did bad? I didn't feel any pain. He wasn't trying to hurt me. He liked it. It felt good to him. I didn't hate it, but I really didn't like it either. Why didn't it feel good to me? What if he wants to do it again? Should I let him? Does this happen between other boys and girls who are friends? I don't know if I should hang out with him anymore, but if I don't, I will be all alone. He told me not to tell. That makes me think that what happened was maybe not a good thing. But if it is supposed to feel good it can't be bad, can it? Maybe if I do it more it will start to feel good for me, too. But I don't know if he will want to do it again. What do I do if he does?

Turned out you did want to do it again. Deep down, I didn't want to, but I did. Mostly because I didn't want you to hate me. And a small part of me wanted to see if it would ever feel good to me like it did to you. I wanted to know what the big deal was about it. So our new "game" continued through the rest of that spring and into summer. Sometimes, we would play the game in the woods but mostly the heat kept us in the basement.

Shortly before the new school year began, I stopped seeing you around the neighborhood, and I never saw you again on the bus—or anywhere else.

I didn't know what had happened to you nor did I care. I was just glad you were gone. and the game was over. I wished I could forget what we had done. But I would never be able to, especially not the way your hands felt on me, the way your mouth felt on me, your musky smell, how you felt in my hands, how you tasted in my mouth.

I should've left your house after you asked me to touch you the first time instead of agreeing. Why didn't I jump off that bed and run home and never return after that first time was over? Was I really that desperate to have a friend?

I guess I was.

Some of the most important choices I would ever have to make for myself were made for me by you before I was even old enough to know what they were or the impact they could have on who I was as a human being. Those choices were:

1. to decide when I was ready to be touched sexually for the first time;
2. to decide whom I wanted that first touch to come from.

By taking those choices from me, you stole my sense of control over my body. And for more than thirty years, I desperately searched for that lost control. Hoping that if I found it, I would be able to erase what you did and take back those choices. But all of my efforts were to no avail. I just ended up making bad, often self-destructive, decisions over and over and over again. The consequences of some of them still haunt me now.

I don't know why you did it. Technically, you were still a kid, but you were old enough to know that what we were doing was wrong, or you wouldn't have told me to keep it a secret.

Because I was so young and you were the first, none of the other sexual predators that followed ever did as much damage as you did.

You destroyed the woman inside me before she could take her first breath.

Chapter 3

Deep Water

It was the summer vacation between fourth and fifth grade. Early one morning, in the early weeks of that academic respite my mother, who usually let me sleep in when there was no school, came into my bedroom calling my name. When I began to stir, she told me to get up and put on my bathing suit. Then, without another word, she turned and left.

I didn't bother to ask why I had to put on my bathing suit. I knew she wouldn't answer until she was good and ready. My mother, for some reason that I never discovered, would make plans without informing the person or persons involved until she absolutely had to, which was almost always at the last minute— allowing no time for any possible arguments.

So on my way to the bathroom, I grabbed the only bathing suit I had; a drab peach-hued one-piece with straps that tied behind my neck. I took a towel from the bathroom closet and headed to the kitchen. As I was finishing my cereal, there was a knock at the breezeway door. It was a girl my age who lived down the road. We were in the same grade, but not in the same class. We did ride the same school bus and sometime during the school year that had just ended we became friends. On the weekends and during breaks, we would hang out. Mostly, I would ride my bike to her house.

I was happy to see her but at the same time confused because I didn't remember making any plans with her for that morning. With puzzlement on my face, I looked from my friend to my mother. Then she informed me that for the next week, I would be going with my friend to a popular local lake, and while there, I would be taking swimming lessons.

Instinctively, my mouth flew open to pro-test because when I was around four years old, I almost drowned in a backyard pool. And while I did not develop a paralyzing fear of water, it did become my least favorite venue. I was able to tolerate being in water as long as my feet were touching bottom. I knew that to learn to swim, I'd have to be out in deep water where my feet couldn't touch, and I wanted no part of that.

However, since I had previously been informed that my feelings didn't matter, I kept my mouth shut.

So, with my towel in hand, I slipped into my cheap rubber drugstore flip-flops and followed my friend out the breezeway to her family's big light-blue rust-spotted van.

As I slid the door shut behind me and sat down, I noticed that my friend's sister and brother, both older, were there. Twenty minutes later, my anxiety, which I kept to myself, about the impending swim lessons, made it seem more like three minutes—the van turned into the parking lot.

There weren't too many people there yet, and we found a spot in the middle of the beach where the sand met the grass to lay out the blanket. Once we were settled, my friend's mom tapped me on the shoulder and pointed to the right end of the beach where I saw a platform sitting out in the water. She said to head over there; my swim lessons were about to start. I turned to my friend to see if she was coming. She told me no, it was just me. I didn't ask why because I didn't really care. Whether she joined me or not, I still had to take the unwanted lessons.

Altogether, there were around ten kids in my swim group, and our first lesson was how to float. I hated every moment, but I had no choice, so I kinda shut down and did what I had to, to get through it. After everyone had taken their turn, the lesson was over, and I headed back to our spot on the beach. My friend and I played in and out of the shallow water until lunchtime then it was time to leave.

The next morning, when I got into the van, the same four people from the day before were present, but today there was an extra. You were sitting in the far back seat next to my friend's brother. The two of you were quietly whispering to each other and grinning as I sat in the middle seat next to my friend and her sister. When we arrived, the boys took off while the girls spread the blankets out. Before I headed out to my swim lesson, I asked my friend who you were, and all she said was your name and that you were a friend of her brother.

The second lesson was all about dog-paddling. Each kid had to dog-paddle for a certain amount of time to pass. And just like the previous lesson, I shut down and plowed through it. There weren't as many kids this time, so the lesson went by quicker. And just like the previous day, once my lesson was over, my friend and I headed to the shallow water to play. But this time, you and her brother had followed us.

I had no idea the actual size or shape of the lake, but as far as I could see, the water's edge was lined by thick groves of various trees. There was a point where both sides curved in forming an incomplete circle like the bottom of an hourglass. A hundred yards or so from the top of the circle was a line of giant bright orange buoys that connected with each side where the trees' lines met the beach. The buoys were connected by a matching rope, and it outlined the outermost barrier of the public swimming area.

You asked if my friend and I wanted to go out and touch the buoys. I knew the water was very deep out there, and I had no interest in touching the buoys. I said the water was too deep, and I hadn't finished swimming lessons yet. You said that was no problem; I could hang on to your shoulders. I had a bad feeling about the whole idea, and I looked at my friend to get her thoughts. The look on her face told me that she wanted to go and that I shouldn't be a chicken. Before I could come up with solid argument against it, my friend had moved behind her brother, placed her hands on his shoulders, and they started out toward the buoys. Not wanting to be called a chicken and made fun of, I caved. I put my hands on your shoulders and let the rest of me hang in the water behind you.

We had gone maybe ten steps toward the buoys when, without warning, your fingers were inside the crotch of my bathing suit. You startled me so badly that, instinctively, I let go of your shoulders. When the water hit my chin and my feet did not touch bottom, I knew I was in real trouble. At that moment, I had no choice but to grab back on to your shoulders. The second I did, your fingers were back inside.

I tried to get away from your hand by letting my body float up on the water's surface, but you had arms like an octopus. So I stretched my body out away from you so that I was only holding on to your shoulders by my fingertips, but that didn't work either. And when I whispered, "Stop," you threatened to leave me out in the deep water to drown.

With my heart thudding out of my chest in fright, I took a look behind me to see if I could tell just how far we were from shore, but there was no way for me to be really sure. However, I was sure we were out far enough that I would not be strong enough to dog-paddle all the way back to shallow water.

So my choices were to either let you continue your filthy revolting explorations or die drowning. I choose the lesser of two evils, although I wasn't really sure which option was worse.

When we all finally did reach the buoys, you reached out with your unoccupied hand and touched it then asked if we were ready to head back. Immediately and emphatically, I piped up, "Yes, let's go back now!" I no longer cared if I was made fun of for being a chicken.

You let out a small low chuckle as you glanced over at the brother, and I saw a knowing look pass between the two of you. Then you both turned and headed back.

The trip in from the buoys was almost exactly the same as the trip out to the buoys; the entire time your fingers relentlessly and, at times painfully, touching. Your hand never broke contact with my vagina. The only difference was that during the trip back toward shore, you walked even slower than you did on the way out. You let the other two get as unsuspiciously far ahead of us as you could so you could have as much time as possible out in the water with your hand between my legs. When I caught on to what you were doing, I came dangerously close to vomiting all over you. After the nausea finally passed, I did the only thing I could. I shut down everything inside me and focused on the beach ahead.

Then at long last, we began to get closer to the other people in the water. And when I thought we were close enough, I dared to let go of your shoulders. I only sank for a half second until the tip of my big toe touched bottom. That was enough for me. I put my other big toe down and kinda like a ballerina, I made my way out from behind you and headed the rest of the way back in on my own. I made my way back to where the blanket was and wrapped myself in my towel. The next thing I knew, it was time to leave. The ride home was quiet. There was none of the usual familiar bantering. I didn't know why, and I didn't care. I just wanted to be out of that van and away from you.

I don't remember much about the rest of that day, just that I changed out of my wet bathing suit, ate lunch, somehow occupied myself until dinner, and went to bed. What I do remember is being afraid, wondering if you were going to be there when I opened the rusty van door in the morning. That fear stayed with me as I fell into a restless sleep that night and was still there when my eyes popped open the next morning. I could feel the fear growing bigger and bigger.

I almost gave an audible sigh of relief when I stepped in the van and saw that you were not there. My friend's brother was not there, either. It was just the girls that day. And it was the same the next day, which was the last day of swimming lessons, where I managed to pass the final test and receive my little paper certificate that said I was officially a swimmer. That day also turned out to be my last at the lake. Once my lessons were completed, my friend never came back to take me to the lake, and I never ever went back that summer or any summer since then.

It was a long time before I saw you again—briefly at a gas station—but I had never forgotten you or what you did to me. You tortured me. You put me in an environment that you knew I couldn't escape from and held me against my will while you sexually assaulted me. And I knew from the look you gave my friend's brother that day that you had been planning to come after me. You showed me abject terror, and I will never forget it.

And all the shame...

I was so ashamed that I let you touch me; I should have taken my chances in the deep water.

I was ashamed for being a coward and not listening to my instincts; I should've never agreed to go.

Because of your actions, the seeds of self-hatred—planted by your predecessors—began to flourish, causing me to feel for the first time ashamed to be alive.

Chapter 4

The Sleepover

I had been invited by your daughter to spend the night. There wasn't enough room for me and her in her twin bed, and I couldn't get comfortable on the hardwood floor, so I ended up sleeping downstairs in the family room on the brown leather couch. It was the middle of the summer I turned twelve, and it was really hot, even at night. I lay down under the thin blanket in my shorts and t-shirt, and the coolness of the leather put me to sleep almost instantly.

Sometime in the middle of the night, a noise brought me out of my slumber. When I opened my eyes and lifted my head, I momentarily forgot where I was. Once my eyes adjusted to the dim moonlight streaming through the windows, I recognized my surroundings and thought that everything was fine and that the house just creaked a little. Just as the back of my head was headed back toward the pillow and my eyes were closing, I heard another noise—like the shuffle of footsteps. I turned my head to the left toward the doorway of the family room. I could make out a shape in the doorway, and though I couldn't tell what it was, I knew it wasn't there when I went to sleep. I felt a little scared and then a little more scared when the shuffling footsteps began again. As the shape stepped into the moonlight, I saw that it was you, and my fear turned into puzzlement.

Why were you here, standing just a few feet away from me in your pajama bottoms and V-neck t-shirt?

I thought that something bad had happened, so I sat up and asked if something was wrong.

"No," you said, "nothing is wrong. I just came down to see if you were okay."

I thought that was odd—but nice. I couldn't remember ever being asked if I was okay.

"Yes, I'm fine," I said as I felt one corner of my mouth go up in a shy half smile.

"Can I have a good night hug?" you asked.

I thought that too was odd, but I didn't see any harm in it. You had always been kind to me. And you were an adult, and I didn't think I had a choice.

I said, "Okay," and stood up from the couch. You took a step forward and bent slightly for me to put my arms around your neck. As my arms went up, I felt your right hand on my back.

I expected to feel your left hand on my back as well, but instead, it made a detour, and I felt it cup and squeeze my right breast.

I froze.

Is this really happening? Again?

I snapped out of it when your hand began to caress my breast. I put my hands on your chest and gave you a shove. It wasn't much, but it was enough for you to drop your hands. Then I crossed my arms over my chest and looked down at the floor.

Why did I do that? I'm not supposed to stop it. But I never expected this from you. You were always nice to me, and now you've ruined it. And I'm pissed about it! But it doesn't matter how I feel. The only thing that matters is that you get what you came down here for. Now, I've made you mad and more determined to get it, and you're really going to hurt me.

So I closed my eyes tightly and tried to steel myself against whatever awful thing was going to happen next. What did happen next was far from what I had expected.

Instead of grabbing me and picking up where you left off, you took a step back. You put your hands up in front of you and said, "I'm sorry. Don't tell anyone. Please don't tell anyone." You kept saying that over and over.

I knew you were waiting for me to say something, but I couldn't talk to you or look at you. I just wanted you to go away! But I knew you wouldn't until I answered, so I said softly, "I won't. I won't tell anyone."

"Are you sure? Do you promise?"

"Yes, I promise. I won't say anything."

I wouldn't have said anything about it even if you hadn't asked me. All the blame would've been heaped on me even though I did absolutely nothing wrong, or did I?

You stood quietly for a moment and then slowly backed out of the room and crept back up the stairs. I stayed where I was standing for a few long moments to make sure you didn't change your mind. When I was relatively sure you weren't coming back, I turned and dove back under the blanket on the couch.

I really wanted to be under the blankets in my own bed, despite not really being safe at home either. But at the moment, it seemed safer than where I was. Besides, my clothes were in my friend's room, and there was no way I was going to go upstairs. And I couldn't be at my house in the morning before everyone woke up. Both families would want to know why I felt I had to walk all the way home in the middle of the night. My mind raced to try and find an acceptable excuse but came up blank. The smarter choice was to stay where I was.

So while still unsure whether or not I was going to be assaulted again, I turned onto my side toward the back of the couch, covered myself from head to toe with the now too-thin blanket, curled up into a ball, and began to tremble violently until I, surprisingly, fell back asleep.

Sometime later, my eyes flew open to strong sunlight streaming in through the basement windows. I sat up quickly when I heard people stirring up in the kitchen. As unobtrusively as I could, I made my way upstairs to my stuff. I jammed my feet in my shoes and grabbed my clothes. With my heart racing, I made my way back downstairs. As I passed the kitchen, I said something about having to be back home first thing in the morning. I didn't even look to see who was there. I spoke just loud enough to be heard as I went out the front door.

I ran the few blocks home in my pajamas. Clothes tucked under my arm. Faster and faster I went trying to outrun the swelling heartache. Heartache from having learned from you that there was no safe place or person for me anywhere in this world.

Chapter 5

Movie Night

It was a humid night a few weeks before my freshman year began. I was at your house hanging out with your two younger sisters. We were getting ready to watch a movie on the TV in the living room. The three of us had made popcorn, spread an old quilt out on the dark blue shag carpet to sit on, and turned off all the lights to make the room more like a movie theater. Your parents had gone upstairs to their bedroom to watch television. You weren't around, so we had the living room to ourselves. We sat down on the quilt with our popcorn and sodas as the movie began. Your sisters were on my left. On my right was a light gray couch. Empty, but it didn't stay that way.

I don't remember what the movie was, but I do remember we were about halfway through when we finished our popcorn. Then all three of us lay down on our stomachs with our heads propped up on pillows to watch the rest. A few minutes later, I heard someone walk in and sit down on the couch. A quick glance to my right showed me it was you who had joined us.

For a brief moment, I was disconcerted, but I quickly dismissed it. I would come to regret not listening to my instincts.

I turned my attention back to the movie. A moment later, I felt something caress my butt. When I realized it was your foot, I froze.

Oh no...

Your sisters were still to my left, engrossed in the movie, and I had to keep it that way.

I had to keep them unaware of what was happening. I knew if you were caught that, ultimately, I would be blamed even though you started it. Things were already bad enough at home, and the last thing I needed was to deal with the fallout from this. See, legally, you were the adult, and I was only fourteen. And in my experience, adults were always innocent, and children were always guilty.

So I laid still and acted engrossed by what was happening on the screen. But the images had gone blurry, and the volume was muffled as if cotton had been stuffed into my ears. The only thing I could focus on was your foot. I hoped that touching my behind would be enough. You continued playing footsie for a while, but then the weight of your foot was gone, and I thought, - hoped that that was the end of it.

My hopes were dashed when your foot returned. Only this time, you slipped it *under* me until it was between my legs. Then you began to rub your toes against me. I had to put a stop to it—somehow. But before I could think of a way to move away from you without drawing attention, something happened that had never happened before.

It began to feel good.

Wrong, wrong, wrong! This is all so wrong! He is not supposed to be touching me, and I am absolutely not supposed to be liking it! This needs to stop, but the truth is a part of me doesn't want it to stop. My body is betraying me. I am fascinated, aroused, and disgusted all at the same time! Physically, it feels so good, but in every other way, it feels so bad. What do I do?

I have no idea how long it went on, but then suddenly, the movie was over. As your sisters began to stir, you quickly withdrew your foot. I quickly stood up and said it was time for me to go home. Without even stopping to help fold the quilt or clean up the popcorn, I began to make my way through the dim house without breaking into a run. Luckily, enough light shone from over the stove that I was able to make my way without running into anything. I knew there was a possibility that you would follow me, but I waited until I had reached the front porch to check. I gently pushed open the storm door, stepped onto the concrete slab of the unlit porch, and turned around. At first, all I saw was the silver metal door, highlighted by the moon, slowly swinging itself shut. I thought I was in the clear, but just as the door was about to latch, it silently swung back open, and you stepped out.

Quickly, you maneuvered yourself in front of me. I was only able to take one small step before I backed into the gray stone wall of the ranch house. You leaned toward me and placed your right hand against the wall level with my head. There was just enough moonlight for me to see your arm blocking my way home and your face about a foot from mine. I heard a slight rustling noise, and then you whispered, "Do you want to touch it?"

For a moment, I was confused, but then I quickly figured out what the rustling noise was and what "it" was. No, I don't want to touch it. That's wrong. But now, I'm not sure, after what happened inside, the way my body reacted.

Before I could even begin to respond, your penis was in my outstretched hand.

What! How? I don't remember lifting my left arm!

I was immobilized. Completely unsure of what I should do or of what you were going to do next. Not a muscle twitched in my entire body as I looked at your shadowed face. When I couldn't stand seeing your face anymore, I felt my eyes shift to my right. You followed my gaze and thought I was looking at the driveway because then you asked if I wanted to get into your car. But I wasn't looking at your car or anything else. I just wanted to escape your glare.

No matter how good my body had felt when we were inside the house, there was no way I was going to get into a car with you. If I did, the only result would be all sorts of incredible pain.

That thought snapped me right out of my trance. I ducked to the left, under your arm, and ran. I ran to my bike that I had dropped in the front yard, jumped on, and raced home down the road with no regard for traffic.

It felt like forever before I finally reached my house. I raced up the driveway and parked my bike in the breezeway. I stood still for a moment to catch my breath and then opened the breezeway door. As I stepped in, I saw my mom to my right, sitting at the kitchen table, reading the newspaper with the small kitchen

TV on. Thankfully, she didn't look up at me as I walked by. I had no idea what my face was showing and couldn't handle any questions. I think I muttered, "Good night," but I don't know if she returned it. I walked as fast as I dared straight down the hall to my bedroom. I flicked the light on, quickly changed into my pajamas, flicked the light off, and jumped into bed. I buried myself under the covers all the way up to my eyes. I lay on my back, staring up at the dark ceiling. I could hear the soft whir of the ceiling fan. Silently, I tried to sort through the events that had just occurred.

I just don't understand why he came after me. I've never given any kind of indication that I wanted him to touch me.

At least I think I haven't…

No, I haven't!

Do I have a target on me somewhere that only they *can see?*

And what was going on with my body? Why did it like it? None of the others had ever made my body feel pleasure. I was being violated. The last thing it should feel like is good!

What is happening to me?

I tried and tried and tried to make sense of it all but was unsuccessful. The arousal and fascination I had felt were gone. But I was still disgusted—and now angry. Angry at you. Angry at my body for betraying me.

You caused my body to commit treason. An act of treason cost me the last little bit of control I had—control over myself, my own person. Never before had I felt so utterly helpless. Subject not only to the malevolent whims of other people; but also to the reactions of my own body.

With that new understanding, I curled into a ball, and stared despondently into the darkness.

Chapter 6

The Tattoo

It was a slushy, overcast January day—Martin Luther King Day, to be exact. I was hanging out that afternoon with a friend that I had gone to high school with, and we were feeling bored and restless. Neither one of us was old enough to buy alcohol yet, and we were trying to come up with something "grown-up" to do—something beyond hanging out and smoking at the mall. About half an hour later, I remembered that there was a tattoo shop one town over. I shared my idea with my friend, and she ardently seconded the motion, so we began making plans.

We grabbed the yellow pages and called to see if the place was open on a holiday—it was. Yay!

Then we asked what the minimum price for a tattoo was and if they took checks. Sixty bucks was the minimum and cash only. The cash-only part threatened to cut our newfound mission short. The banks were closed for the holiday, and neither one of us was sure if we had enough on hand. She went up to her bedroom to check her stash, and I went home to check mine. I said that I would call her when I had a total.

I retrieved my stash from the back of my underwear drawer and found that I only had forty-one bucks. I grabbed my small brass piggy bank with blue rhinestone eyes and dumped the contents onto my bed. I then scrounged through my car and my purse but could only come up with another three dollars in change. Damn. Sixteen short. I didn't want to scrap the tattoo plan just yet, so I sat on the edge of my bed and, with the whispering sound of the small pile of change sliding toward me, I weighed my limited options.

I could ask my parents for the twenty bucks, but I wasn't sure if it would be worth it. See, I was always told that when I became an adult, I could make my own decisions. What I was not told is that there would continue to be— like when I was a minor—repercussions for any decisions made by me that they didn't like.

I knew they would absolutely not like the tattoo idea. And I knew that they wouldn't care if I was over eighteen; they would lay into me. The very last thing I wanted was yet another berating about how stupid and worthless I was. I could lie and tell them something they'd accept, but that could be a daunting task and I really didn't want to go there.

Then there was my brother. Now, my baby brother was a notorious tattle-tale, and his singing had gotten me into a lot of trouble, so I was hesitant. But I was also desperate.

At the time, I did not know why I was so desperate for that tattoo. Looking back now, I think part of the reason was my impulsiveness and tenacity. And I believe that the biggest part of that reason was that I saw it as a way to gain back some control. I made the decision to get the tattoo, therefore, I was the one in control of my body.

I didn't like either of my choices, but I had a feeling that I should try my brother first.

My brother and I were the only ones home, so before the parents returned, I called my brother into my room. I told him my plan, what I needed, and I promised I would go to the bank the very next day and pay him back. Without hesitation, he told me he did have enough cash, and he would let me borrow it, but on one condition—I had to let him come with us.

I told him absolutely not, that there was no way that he would be able to resist telling Mom and Dad a whopper like this!

He promised he wouldn't tell. He put his palms together in front of him as if in prayer and bounced on the balls of his feet while swearing up and down that he would say a word.

I thought it over for a moment or two.

I really, really wanted a tattoo, and the truth was that even if he did tattle, in the end, there would be nothing my parents could do about the tattoo itself, so yeah, I'll take my chances.

So I looked my little brother straight in the eyes and promised him that he would be very sorry if was lying to me. He swore some more that he wouldn't tell, and he had what appeared to be an earnest look on his face, so I told him he could go. He broke out such a wide joyful grin I couldn't help but smile a little myself.

He picked his wallet up from his desk and handed me a twenty, and then I called my friend and told her I had enough cash and that I had to bring my brother with me. She said she was also able to come up with the cash, and she was fine with my brother tagging long, and she would pick us up after dinner.

During dinner, I told my parents I was going to the mall with my friend. My brother asked my parents if he could go with us. They said that was fine, and we quickly finished eating, so we would be ready when it was time to leave. Shortly after I had finished washing the dishes, there was a splash of headlights across half the kitchen as my friend pulled into the driveway. As soon as my brother and I got into the car, we all started chatting excitedly and nervously about the adventure ahead of us—possible tattoo choices, how big we wanted them, where on our bodies would we get them, how much would it hurt, and etc. All of us were in high spirits—I so much so that I even let my brother smoke one of my cigarettes.

Less than fifteen minutes later, we pulled into the parking lot next to the tattoo shop. Quickly but carefully, we crossed the cold slushy blacktop to a boxy two-story white house. There was no sign of life on the second floor, but the main floor was warmly lit behind the large front windows that spanned the whole front side of the house that were plastered with a few posters—Led Zeppelin, Pink Floyd, Def Leppard; a couple poster boards covered in, what I interpreted to be, ready-made tattoos for choosing, and a bright red neon sign that glowed OPEN. Upon entering, I saw you, the only other person in the shop besides us three, standing next to a glass display counter with a greasy salt-and-pepper mullet and an equally oily salt-and-pepper moustache and beard, wearing a faded black T-shirt, well-worn jeans, and old black work boots.

We hung our coats on a weathered wooden rack standing near the front door.

Then you asked which one(s) of us was getting a tattoo and did we know what we wanted. My friend and I raised our hands in unison and said we were the ones getting a tattoo, and no, we weren't sure yet what we wanted. So you showed us a pile of photo albums we could look through for ideas. They all contained pictures similar to the poster boards in the window, and you told us the pre-drawn pictures were called "flash." I grabbed an album off the top of the pile and began to leaf through. There were so many options that I didn't think I would be able to choose. Then on one of the last pages of the album, I found it. It was a little bigger than a quarter and would fit perfectly where I wanted it. I showed you the one I wanted and asked how much it would be. Sixty bucks. Perfect. You asked where I wanted it, and I pointed to the left side of my chest above my breast and slightly toward my armpit.

I chose that spot because the tattoo would be better hidden—yes, mainly from my parents—under my shirt. And besides, my tattoo was my business and mine to show if I chose to.

Then you said I would have to change my shirt. I told you I specifically wore this shirt, a white button-down oxford, because it would be easy to unbutton just a couple and move it and my bra strap out of the way. You countered with how you couldn't be responsible for any ink and/or blood getting on my clothes. I asked if you were serious. You said yes, there was something for me to put on in the bathroom and that you wouldn't do the tattoo unless I put it on. I mulled it over as I turned to my companions for consultation and they both just looked at me with quick shrugs that said, "It's up to you," so no help there. But I badly wanted that tattoo

I thought it would give me back some sense of control over my body

and my tenacity was overriding the warning signs that my instincts were flashing, so I asked where the bathroom was.

I found a purple stretchy halter top hanging on a hook on the back of the bathroom door. Grimacing a little, I took off my shirt and bra and quickly replaced it with the god-knows-who's-worn-this halter top before I could change my mind. I took a deep breath as I stepped out of the cramped industrial bathroom. Looking straight ahead, I made a beeline to the tattoo chair and sat down, blushing in embarrassment, but determined to walk out of there with a tattoo.

It turned out not to be nearly as painful as I thought it would be, and it only took about fifteen minutes, which I was grateful for because I wanted out of that halter top ASAP.

When you were done tattooing, you said all you had to do was wipe off the excess ink and blood and put a gauze pad over it. Then you sprayed soapy water on a folded paper towel and cleaned off my new tattoo. When you were done, you dropped the wet inky paper towel to the floor then took that same now-empty hand, plunged it under the halter top, firmly grabbed my left breast, and then pulled your hand out. It happened so fast and so unexpectedly that I couldn't have stopped you if I tried.

I looked at you, mouth hanging open in astonishment. You looked right back into my eyes with a sleazy grin on your face that said, "Gotcha." I was speechless. My friend and brother had seen what had happened and only gave brief but nervous giggles—the kind of giggles that a lot of people let out when something unexpected and unpleasant occurs and they are not sure how to react.

Then I looked down at where my tattoo was, and you had already taped gauze over it and was telling me I was done. I flew out of the chair and wordlessly hurried back to the bathroom. I tore off the nasty halter top and put my bra and shirt back on as fast as I could. I was numb. When I came out, you had already started tattooing my friend. Her tattoo was the same size as mine, but not in the same place. She had chosen to get hers on the inside of her ankle.

I knew her parents would more than likely freak out over a tattoo, like mine would, and I thought she was so brave to get it in such an easy-to-see area. And at that moment, I very much wished that I had been as brave.

Nobody looked at me when I returned, and nothing was said about what you had done to me. There was some chit-chat during my friend's tattoo, but I didn't say a thing. I just stood there next to my brother looking at the tattoo forming on her ankle but not really seeing it. I felt like I was watching a scene from a movie, but at the same time, I was cast member *in* that same scene.

I had lost the sense of time, and the next thing I remember was walking out of your shop to the car. The cold air was bracing, and I took in a huge gulp, as if I'd been suffocating. My brother and my friend hurried out to the car, but I lagged behind a little, wanting a few more unconfined moments in the clean cold air.

The ride home was subdued compared to the ride to the tattoo shop. We just listened to the radio without talking. That was fine with me because I wasn't sure I could hold up my end of any conversation. Especially if the conversation turned to what you had done to me. I couldn't even *think* about it, let alone talk about it. At the time, I couldn't have put a word to why that was the case but now I know.

I was in shock.

However, it didn't take long for the shock to wear off and my brain—of its own volition—to begin processing the events of that evening. I did not want to think about it; I didn't see the need to because what you did to me was very familiar. But there was also an element present that I hadn't experienced before.

I was used to public humiliation, but it had always only come from physical and verbal abuse.

However, I had never before been sexually abused in public, and the humiliation was compounded by it happening right in front of people that I *knew*.

That was a whole new level of humiliation that I didn't know could exist.

And the pain from that kind of humiliation was…indescribable. And it went beyond mental and emotional. At one point, it got so bad that it manifested into a sharp stabbing physical pain in my gut.

I also learned more than just a new level of humiliation from you that night.

See, up until the moment you grabbed me, I had believed that because I was now an adult, my appeal to sexual predators—which I had assumed was only due to my childness—would be lost.

You showed me that it didn't matter how old I was or where I was or who was around; there would always be someone out there... hunting me.

Chapter 7

Mom

What were you thinking? Seriously? Hang on to your purse strap? We were downtown in a crowded stadium full of strangers. I was only five years old. Five! I wasn't able to be responsible for myself. And even if I hadn't let go, anyone could have come along and grabbed me, and you wouldn't have even noticed because of all the jostling while trying to maneuver through the throng of people. What would you have done if I had truly disappeared? I wonder because your reaction after I was found was not right. You completely ignored me for the rest of the night. On our way to the car in the coliseum parking lot, driving to the restaurant, while we were at the restaurant, driving home—you didn't say a word. You never even looked at me.

And when we got home, you kept to the kitchen. Cleaning and piddling around while less than six feet away from you, your husband was brutalizing your daughter. How could you listen to me screaming and just let it go on and on?

The next morning was more of the same. Not a word from you. Just barely a glance in my direction. But that glance said it all. It told me that you blamed me for getting lost when I wasn't really lost—you failed to keep track of me. And that I deserved everything I had gotten the night before.

When I was a small child, someone had given me a little blue journal with an imprint of a girl dressed like a Holly Hobbie doll on the cover. That journal sat untouched until after the sexual abuse began. One day, I picked it up, sat in the chair at the desk in my bedroom, and drew pictures of what had happened to me.

I don't know what prompted me to put those images on paper. Maybe I just needed to get it out of my head to try to make some sense out of it. After I finished, I wasn't sure if I should keep them or destroy them right away, so I just stuffed the journal way back in one of my desk drawers.

A few evenings later, as soon as I turned off the water and began stepping out of the basement shower, you came flying down the steps. You had my little blue journal and were waving it around with a crazed look on your face.

"What is this? Why did you do this?" you yelled.

At first, I just stood there, naked and shivering, wide eyed with disbelief, staring at my journal that you were now waving in my face, while fumbling for a towel to wrap around myself.

As I stood there trembling, not just with the cold but also with fear, struggling to get control of the towel, my mind raced to try to answer your questions—questions that took me wholly by surprise.

Why are you so angry? Do you think I just came up with those images out of thin air? How can you not see that these things have happened to me? Why aren't you asking if someone is touching me where they shouldn't? Why aren't you asking me if someone is hurting me? Why am I the bad guy?

Your startling and unexpected reaction to what you had found told me that if I told you the truth about the origins of those drawings, you would blame it all on me, and I didn't think I'd be able to survive the punishment.

Again and again, you kept on.

"What is this?"

"Why did you do this?"

I knew I couldn't stall any longer. Words needed to come out of my mouth. All I could say was, "I don't know! I'm sorry!"

"Why did you do this?"

"I don't know! I don't know! I'm sorry! I'm sorry! I'm sorry!"

In my shock and confusion, that was the only answer I could muster.

When you realized that was all you were going to get out of me, you backed off. But before you went back upstairs, you handed me the journal and told me menacingly, "Get rid of this, and I don't ever want to see anything like this ever again." Then you left me standing there clutching the towel around me, staring at the blue book in my hand, feeling every bit a worthless, nasty, nine-year-old little piece of shit.

There are a couple of things I need to clarify about one of the events that took place when I was thirteen:

1. I didn't try to kill myself just to get attention. I was in pain—intolerable, soul-wrenching pain—and I just wanted it to stop. Between the phys-

ical, mental, and verbal abuse and indifference I had to live with at home and the sexual predators outside the house, I was at the end of my rope. I had no means to deal with any of it, and I couldn't find any other way to get away from it. I was dying from the inside out. Why let it go on any longer?

2. Why did I take all those pills at school instead of at home? Because "home" was an enormous part of the problem! If I had been able to get what I needed from my parents, I wouldn't have had to make such a drastic move. So I overdosed at school with a sliver of hope that maybe, just *maybe*, one of the adults there would care just enough to at least try to help me. As far as I could see, it was the only option left.

I didn't want to die, and I didn't want to live. I had become depleted and desperate.

To hell with it. At the least, I have a fifty-fifty chance because death is a guarantee that the pain will stop.

When what I had done was discovered, an ambulance was called. I was at the hospital for quite a few hours, and not once did the doctor or the nurses or you or Dad ask me why I had tried to commit suicide. Nor did any of you look at me—not a glance. The only thing that was looked at were the machines that were monitoring my vitals.

Once we got home, the only time you did look at me was to tell me that the school principal had phoned to say I was suspended from school for two weeks, and I was required to see a psychiatrist once a week for the next few months. Then you began yelling at me about how much money that was going to cost you, how much of an inconvenience I was because you were going to have to take time out of your schedule to take me to these appointments, and how awful it would be for you if anyone found out what I had done.

Are you kidding me? I tried to kill myself, and all you care about is how it affects you?

I was still alive and I thought that maybe this was my chance to get some help. Maybe...

There we were, Mom, on our way to my first mandatory counseling session. I could feel your anger and resentment radiating from you in giant waves. It filled the entire cab of the dark-blue-and-silver pick-up truck and displaced all the oxygen. I could barely breathe. And that's the way it was going to and coming from every single trip to the counseling office. Your hatred was pressing me back into and immobilizing me against the truck's blue bench seat. Even though we lived less than fifteen minutes from the counseling center, those were, to this day, the longest and most arduous automobile rides of my life. I had no choice but to endure it, but I told myself it would be okay because I was finally going to get some answers. The biggest and most important question that had been plaguing me for so long was "Am I going insane?"

The doctor stepped into the waiting room and called my name. I stood up to follow him, and so did you.

Why did she stand up? Does she think she's going with me?

Much to my chagrin, that's exactly what you thought. And you did, ignoring the identical looks of puzzlement on my face and the doctor's. At first, I thought—hoped—the doctor would say something that would cause you to stay in the waiting room, but he kept quiet as he led us back to his office.

The right side of his office was all overflowing bookshelves. On the left, a desk and chair. And in the middle of the room, a mustard-colored vinyl loveseat and armchair facing each other. The doctor indicated my mother and I sit on the loveseat while he settled into the armchair.

For the first minute or so, we all sat in silence. The look on the doctor's face made me wonder if he was thinking the same thing I was, "Is my mother going to sit in on the entire session?" When I couldn't stand the tension-soaked silence anymore, I timidly asked you that very question. With an incredulous look, you burst out, "Of course I am! You're not going to talk about our family without me here!"

My head dropped, and my heart sank as my first-ever hope for some kind of delivery from the hell I was in shrank into nothingness before me. Like the little spot of light that came on the center screen of an old console television after it was turned off, it grew smaller and smaller until it blinked out of existence, and all that was left was a big black empty space.

I looked imploringly at the doctor to see if he was going to do anything about it, but I could tell by his expression that he wasn't going to do a thing.

After a few minutes of more tense silence, the doctor asked me why I was there. I waited a moment to see if you were going to answer for me. But you just sat there, purse on your lap with a death grip on its handles, staring straight ahead beyond the doctor, at the wall behind him and his desk. So head down, embarrassed, I softly answered, "Because I took a bunch of pills at school."

"Can you tell me why?" asked the doctor.

With my head still down, I cast a brief sideways glance at you then shrugged my shoulders.

No, I can't tell you why because part of the "why" is sitting right next to me. My mother, waiting to thwart anything I say that could cast her or her husband—my father—in a bad light. See, she knows. Deep down, she knows that Dad's abuse has done something to me. And I wouldn't be surprised if, somewhere in the back of her mind, she realizes that I have been sexually abused as well. But I don't think she knows how to handle either situation. And because of that, she lives in a state of silent denial. What she doesn't understand is that her silence is just as hard, if not harder, on me than anything else.

Knowing that I couldn't say what I was thinking, I kept my mouth shut, and the rest of the hour-long appointment continued in strained silence.

Occasionally when my neck would begin to stiffen, I would hesitantly lift my head and look around the room with only my eyes, trying not to turn any attention onto myself by moving my head. When my gaze would land on the doctor, his head was usually down. Periodically, he would shift in his mustard chair, adjust his glasses, or move his pen around on his yellow legal pad. If our eyes did happen to meet, I could see my disappointment and frustration reflected in his eyes. Not a word was spoken by the three of us until it was time for the doctor to announce that our time was up.

And that's how each and every session went for the next three months—with you sitting on that ugly condiment-colored love seat, fiercely clutching your purse on your lap, staring at the wall, pursing your lips in anger. And me sitting next to you, staring down at my fingernails.

You refused to help me yourself. And after that first session, when I realized that you would never let anyone else help me either, I felt sorry that my suicide attempt was unsuccessful—I wanted to die more than ever.

———————◆———————

You did nothing. All those times when Dad's anger got out of hand, you would avert your eyes in silence—leaving me to absorb all of his rage.

And afterward, you continued to do nothing. Never once was there a comforting touch. Never a sympathetic look. Not even one quiet word to tell me that it wasn't my fault.

Now I know I made mistakes, and there were times when it was my fault. But not *every* time. More often than not, I had nothing to do with it and you knew that.

I was bewildered by your indifference toward me. I tried hard to figure out the reason for that indifference and could come up with only one that made sense to me.

You thought of me as a burden. Just like Dad. And just like Dad, you resented me for being born too soon after your marriage.

Chapter 8

Giving Back the Shame

Shame, noun: the painful feeling arising from the consciousness of something dishonorable, improper, ridiculous, etc. done by oneself or another.

(Dictionary.com)

E very person on the planet has shame. It's an essential component of being human. Some accumulate a great deal of shame and others not so much, but we all have it to some degree. And the majority of humans probably first learned about shame as children. Remember, our parents saying, "You should be ashamed of yourself" when we did something wrong?

All of my most shameful moments I brought onto myself because of my bad decisions. And every one of those moments were an attempt to escape the shame that was put upon me because of your bad decisions.

I had a lot of sex, mostly with strangers and mostly unprotected. When a warm body wasn't available, I turned to pornography. After a while, those warm bodies turned into more of a hassle than they were worth, and I ended up with a porn addiction.

There were drugs; I took anything I could smoke, snort, or ingest whenever I could get my hands on it.

I even tried rock-and-roll. At one time, I worked in the radio industry, and at the time, I thought I had found my "calling." So, I tried to escape by surrounding myself with that whole scene.

Most of my attempts to escape worked so far as the effects were always temporary. And every time the effects wore off, I was left with even more shame of my own making, that I could only add to the shame that I had already received from you. Each bad decision I made piled on more and more shame until I was all but pulverized by it.

Sometimes, when my attempts to escape failed, I would slam my head against a wall until I couldn't take it. Either on the side or the back, so if I got a bruise or a lump or split my scalp open, it wouldn't be seen under my hair.

Then came a time that the pain from all the shame got so intense that my body and my brain would suddenly seize up like a dry engine. And when that happened, I couldn't speak, could barely move, and my breathing all but stopped. I couldn't think of where I was or remember my own name.

The first time this happened, I became panicky and didn't know what to do at first. Then I had an idea—like in the movies, when someone freezes up and another person gives them a good hard smack across the face to snap them out of it. I'd fight pain with pain. Since there wasn't anyone around to smack me, I needed an alternate solution. I was able to reach into my pants pockets and among the flotsam I found a plastic lighter and a large paper clip. I unfolded one side of the paper clip into a *L* and heated it up until it was glowing red. I then pressed it to the nearest exposed skin, the inside of my elbow, and I held it there until I smelled my own burning flesh.

It worked. The burning pain killed the shame pain.

That was not the only time I was forced to take those measures.

And occasionally, the thoughts of suicide would return. There were quite a few times that I gave it more than serious thought. And one time, I got dangerously close…again.

And that is my shame. Not all of it, but the worst of it. And all those bad decisions were influenced by the things you did to me. Just like a lot of your bad decisions were probably influenced by the bad decisions that other people made in your life.

And it's important for you to know that this is not about assigning blame. I am as much to blame for my own shame as you are for yours. I'm not looking for any kind of apology. I'm not even mad anymore.

This is strictly about who's *shame* it is. For decades, I've been crumbling under the weight of not just my shame but yours, as well, and I'm not going to live with that pain anymore. I will no longer bear the responsibility for your actions.

And there was only one way for me to be free from it.

It all started when I came to a time in my life where I was unable to escape from my shame. Everything I tried was utterly useless. The pain became so unbearable that, after exhausting all resources available to me, I turned to the only one left that I hadn't touched—God.

I had not reached out to God before because I thought I was entirely too broken to fix. I still thought that when I did ask God for help, but I was in so much pain that I had to take the chance.

After I pleaded with God for help, He brought some other people into my life that could guide me on my quest with Him to find an end to my shame.

One person in particular had an enormous impact on me, my relationship with God, and my journey—but that's a whole other story.

From those people, I learned that I could find everything I needed to end my shame-pain through God; I just had to get to know Him.

So I began to work on my relationship with God. I prayed a lot, read the Bible, found a church, and made a conscious effort when the ugly negative thoughts pop into my mind—that were usually about myself—to immediately replace them with positive thoughts, like time spent with my nieces or the book I was reading. Any random thought worked as long as it was non-negative.

As time passed, I felt my relationship with God begin to deepen and grow stronger. Then for some reason not yet known to me, came the moment I realized that, not only had that relationship plateaued, but all my shame pain was still there. Then this word popped into my head, Forgive. Over and over. Forgive.

I immediately knew that word was coming from God, but I didn't want any part of it. In my mind, to forgive meant that I would be saying, "Don't worry about it. It's perfectly okay that you abused me," and then just smile and move on because there's nothing I can do about it anyway. No way was I going to do that!

But still, that blasted word kept coming back...

Forgive. Forgive. Forgive. Forgive.

Softly but insistently flashing behind my eyes.

I tried and tried to ignore it, to no avail. And eventually, I caught on that God was not going to drop the whole Forgive thing, so I gave in, but not right away. First, I did research on Forgive just to be sure that my understanding of the word was, indeed, correct.

I consulted numerous dictionaries, pastors, and the Bible. I found that they all said pretty much the same thing regarding Forgive. I also found that my understanding of the word was wrong.

In a nutshell, the word Forgive means to stop feeling angry with someone who has done something wrong. My anger with you was caused by the shame that you put on me. So for me to stop feeling angry, I had to do something about that shame. I had to give it back to you. You were the one who created it: therefore, it belongs to you.

So to give you back your shame...

"I forgive you."

Chapter 9

Shame, Forgiveness, and Me

I remember clearly when I first forgave. I couldn't come up with an argument against what I had discovered about forgiveness, and God was relentless, so I did it.

One morning during my shower, I closed my eyes, tilted my head back, and loudly declared, "I forgive all of you."

Then I said each person's name.

"And I forgive myself."

As the last word left my lips, there was a short thunder-like CRACK that sounded like it came from right there in the shower, but I saw nothing that could've been the source of the sound that I distinctly heard. I didn't know what or if it meant anything, but what happened after meant everything.

I was overcome by this joy—a pure, unadulterated joy that I had never felt before in my life. So much so that I began to cry. Then I started laughing. Then out loud, I thanked

God for that gift of joy. And I stood there under the hot water, crying, laughing, and thanking God all at the same time, until the shower ran freezing cold.

My forgiving them and forgiving me was what I needed to do mentally, emotionally, spiritually, and physically to release myself from the burden of all the shame—theirs and mine. From that very moment on, I stopped living as a prisoner.

However, my shame was relentless. In no time it was back, trying to lock me up and resume command. It would bully its way in and make itself right back at home. I have to admit, more so when I was new to forgiveness and trusting God, that it was easy for the shame to get to me. Shame had been in command for the first four decades of my life, so it was no surprise that I would forget that I had indeed escaped it. But once I did realize that the shame and its pain were back, I would pray in earnest to God, asking for help to remember that I trust Him, that I have forgiven and been freed from the shame, and that I'm not a prisoner anymore. And that is exactly what God did.

Every time the shame came back, God was there, reminding me. Sometimes it just took longer for me to hear Him. And every time I shook off the shame, the joy, along with peace and love, would come rushing in. At times, they were so stunning and overpowering that I couldn't help but smile or burst into tears or dance around or simply jump up and down, yelling, "Thank You!"

Sometimes everything all at once.

Those times when shame returned were crucial to my relationship with God because He did show up every time I needed Him, and every time my trust in Him deepened. And the more I trusted Him. the more joy, peace, and love there was. And the reappearances of shame became shorter and less frequent. To this day, the shame still tries to insinuate itself, and I expect it will continue to until I die, but I don't worry because I know that it will only bring me and God closer to each other.

Anger, guilt, envy, self-hatred, sadness, and mistrust are the biggest components of my shame. That's the life I was trapped in. And my shame was a constant companion. It was painful and isolating. Now I know that there were a lot of other people on the planet who had been abused, but among all the people in my own circle, I was the only one that I knew of who had. Abuse is not exactly a subject that comes up in everyday conversation.

The isolation very much narrowed and darkened my point of view of everything. All I could see was that everybody was getting what they wanted. And since I was taught that what I wanted didn't matter, all I ever got was shame.

I hated myself. I hated people. I hated the world.

God changed all of that for me. Before Him, I had never experienced joy, peace, or love, not in any real or true way. Gradually, the isolation faded away, and as it did, my viewpoint began to expand and brighten. Slowly but surely, I am learning that my feelings do matter.

I don't hate myself or people or the world anymore.

I have genuinely begun to love myself. And the more I love myself, the more love I am able to give to other people. It's the same with my relationship with God. As it grows stronger, my love for God deepens, which facilitates my ability to pass that love on and share the amazing gifts I've received in that love.

I'd love to say that since I let go of the shame that everyday has been all puppies and sparkles, but of course, that would be a lie. I still do and will continue to have bad days. But now, I'm much better at handling those because God is always there. And on occasion, one or more of those days have been, and will be, horrendous. On those days, I have been known to start doubting my relationship with God. When I sense that happening, I think of my favorite Bible verse:

> "For I know the plans I have for you," declares the Lord, "plans to prosper you and not to harm you, plans to give you hope and a future."

Jeremiah 29:11 (NIV)

There are four specific words in that verse that pull me out of the doubt every time—

"not to harm you"

Those words struck me like lightening the first time I read them. They have been an enormous part of repairing my soul ever since.

"plans to give you hope and a future."

My whole life, no one has ever given me either of those. Now God has blessed me with both. I could thank Him until the end of time, and it would never be enough to express my gratitude.

And I know that I will continue to, at times, make bad decisions and create new shame for myself. I am, after all, still an imperfect being. The difference now is that I don't let myself get stuck in the shame anymore. As long as I live my life with God, I am free—free to live a real, positive, meaningful life.

I have access to all the joy, peace, and love I want and need. I never had those things, not in any true and real way, until I moved the shame out to make room for God.

Prior to God, my only aspiration was to escape my shame by becoming as numb as I possibly could. Now that I understand that my relationship with God is the most important part of my life, I have a much different desire.

I want to become the person God wants me to be, and I pray that during that process— as I continue on my journey with God—I can help other people free themselves from the shame.

When you pass through
the waters,
I will be with you;
and when you pass
through the rivers,
they will not sweep over you.
When you walk through the fire,
you will not be burned;
the flames will not set you ablaze.
For I am the Lord your God,
the Holy One of Israel, your Savior.

—Isaiah 43:2-3 (NIV)

Thank you, God

Thank you, Shawn, my wonderful husband

Thank you, Wm. Paul Young

Thank you,
Nick Anderson
Lynn Bates
Wally Bates
Sabrina Beard
Leslie Black
Dr. Roy Fouch
Aunt Janet Kipp
Karin Maney
Andy Rainey
Aunt Lynne Stroup
Michelle Vondrell
Donna Workman
Maura Workman

Be strong and courageous. Do not be afraid or terrified because of them, for the Lord your God goes with you; he will never leave you nor forsake you.

—Deuteronomy 31:6 (NIV)

About the Author

Stacey Workman was born and raised in Deerfield Township, Ohio. She still resides in the greater Cincinnati area with her husband and two dogs.

If you are interested in connecting with Stacey, please email her at swbook2019@gmail.com.

9 781645 156710